Howie and Bede both have growling monster motorbikes.

"Howie's is grey, but mine's better cos it's red"

jokes Bede.

"No mine's better"

sniggers Howie.

They always polish them till they sparkle then can't wait to take them for a ride and get them muddy again.

"Let's go to Europe!"

"Yeah! We can ride all day
and sleep in our tent when
we get tired."

They pack their tent,
socks and spare undies
and jump on
their bikes.

"Wow wow!! Wow wow!!" the bikes roar with excitement.

It takes hours and hours to reach the ferry port.

"Huff! This is really boring, when do we get to Europe!"

"UUUAAAAHHHHHHH-
AAAAAAHHHH"
yawns Bede.

They sleep all the way as the choppy sea teases with the playful ship.

"Wow wow!! Wow wow!! Careful"

shriek the bikes

"Germans drive on the
wrong side of the road"

"Kneeoww!! Out of the way!!" grumbles the Porsche.

"And drive fast too!"

They wind their
way through the
cool dark forest until
they see glimmers of
snow-capped mountains
glistening under the smile of the moon.

"UUUAAAAHHHHHHH-AAAAAAHHHH" **yawns Howie.**

"Too tired to put up the tent"

Zonk! Out like a light, nested next to the bikes.

Howie wakes early the next morning with dew dripping from his nose.

"Yew!" smiles Bede.

"Is mine dribbling too"

"Yeap!" nods Howie with a broad grin.

"Wow wow!! Wow wow!! Careful, it's starting to rain!" warn the bikes.

It tips down all day long, getting wetter and wetter.

"UUUAAAA-HHHHHHHAAA-AAAHHHH" yawns Bede.

"Too wet to put up the tent" he sighs.

They huddle balanced on a thin bench in the shower block, slowly joined by more and more noisy drenched campers.

Still raining next morning. *"Wow wow!! Wow wow!! Let's go to Italy, it's sunny there"* **sneer the bikes.**

With the mountains behind them and the sun in their face they begin to feel drowsy.

"*UUUAAAAHHHHHHH-AAAAAAHHHH*"
yawns Howie
"*time to stop*"

Hungry after a nap

"*What do we eat in Italy!*"
questions Howie.

"*Pizza and Spaghetti, yum!*"

Holding up two fingers, they point at the menu.

"Pizza and Spaghetti, per favore"

With four plates in front of them, they giggle and dump the spaghetti on the pizza .....

....and cram down the lot.

"UUUAAAAHHHHHHHH-AAAAAAHHHHH, let's put up the tent" **yawns Howie.**

Bang, bang, bang!
Bang bang bang!

All the tent pegs lie bent next to the hammer.

"Too hard to put up the tent!"

Nice and warm and dry, they snooze
till morning leaving the tent
in a messy heap.

"Look Howie, no dribbles"
say Bede pointing at his nose.

"*Wow wow!! Wow wow!!*

Let's go to France" **encourage the bikes.**

"**Beep beep!!**" **oinks a red Ferrari.**

"**Not going anywhere,**

but in a hurry.

Vrum vrum!!"

It gets hotter and

hotter, leaving Italy for France.

Enjoying the weather and after a relaxing trek.

"Wow wow!! Cough cough!!"
choke the bikes.

"How's your fuel Howie"

"U-Oh! Running on fresh air!"

They switch off their engines and
cruise down the mountain mimicking the growl of the bikes,
"Wow Wow", all the way to the petrol station.

Raising 10 fingers, Bede holds out his money and watches the counter. 6,7,8,9...

"Stop! I'm full up!" eeks the bike.

"Dix, ten" sniggers the pump man.

"Gurrhh! That's very naughty" Bede tells the man.

Full of fuel they journey to Paris

through rolling hills shadowed by fluffy clouds.

"What do we eat in France?"

"Um... Frogs and snails"

"Yuck! Fancy Chinese?" asks Howie

and they picnic under the gaze of the Eiffel tower.

"UUUAAAAHHHHHHH-AAAAAAHHHH!

Just right to put up the tent"

"Wow wow!! Wow wow!! Time to aim home"

lament the bikes.

Riding along the long straight highways,

speckles of rain darken the road.

Speckles start to splash. Splashes turn to puddles.

"Wow wow!! Cough cough!!" **choke the bikes.**

"Running on fresh air?"

"No!! Wow!! Cough!! Don't like the rain!" **complain the bikes.**

They stop under a bridge and wait for the weather to brighten.

The sun burns back the clouds and a rainbow circles the sky.

At the port they take a hover craft which zips across the water.

Back home.

"UUUAAAAHHHHHHH-AAAAAAHHHH,

shall we put up the tent?"

yawns Bede

"Nope, I want to snuggle in my own bed tonight!"

Printed in Great Britain
by Amazon